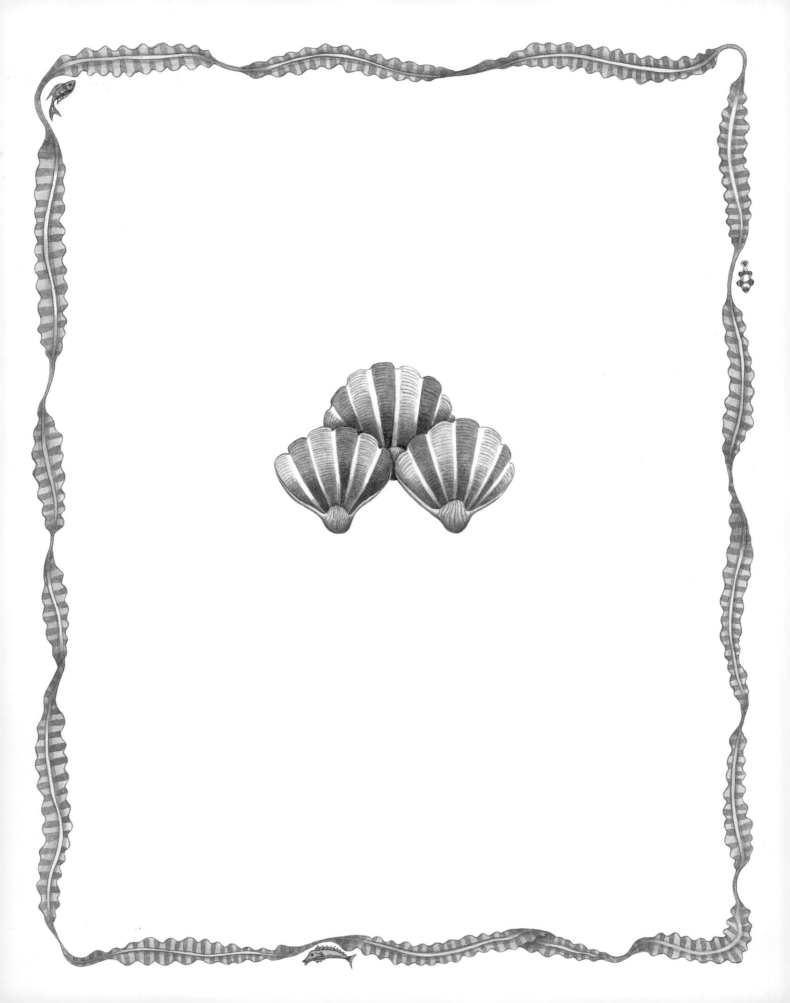

·T·H·E·
MERMAID
and Other Sea Poems

Compiled and Illustrated by
SOPHIE WINDHAM

SCHOLASTIC
HARDCOVER

SCHOLASTIC INC.
NEW YORK

ACKNOWLEDGMENTS

The compiler and publishers wish to thank all the poets, agents and publishers and other copyright holders who kindly granted us permission to use the poems in this anthology.

"Whale" by Geoffrey Dearmer reprinted by permission of the author and The Society of Authors as his representative. "Do Oysters Sneeze?" by Jack Prelutsky from *New Kid on the Block* published by William Heinemann Ltd., reprinted by permission of Reed International Books. "Seahorse" by Blake Morrison from *Casting a Spell* published by Orchard Books, reprinted by permission of the author. "Grim and Gloomy" by James Reeves from *The Wandering Moon and Other Poems* published by Puffin Books, reprinted by permission of the James Reeves Estate. "My Other Granny" by Ted Hughes from *Meet My Folks!* published by Faber and Faber Ltd., reprinted by permission of the publishers. "The Mermaid" and "The Eel" by Ogden Nash from *Verses From 1929 On* published by André Deutsch Ltd. Copyright 1942, 1944 by Ogden Nash. "Ocean Diners" by J. Patrick Lewis from *Two-Legged, Four-Legged, No-Legged Rhymes* copyright 1991 J. Patrick Lewis, reprinted by permission of Joanna Lewis Cole. "The Dolphin" by Alan Bold from *A Very First Poetry Book* ed. John Foster published by Oxford University Press, reprinted by permission of the author. "Undersea" by Marchette Chute from *Piper, Pipe That Song Again!* compiled by Nancy Larrick, copyright © 1965 by Random House, Inc. Reprinted by permission of Elizabeth Roach. "The Flattered Flying Fish" by E. V. Rieu from *The Flattered Flying Fish and Other Poems* published by Methuen Children's Books, reprinted by permission of Richard Rieu. "Narwhal" by X.J. Kennedy from *Did Adam Name the Vinegaroon*. Text copyright © 1982 by X. J. Kennedy. Reprinted by permission of David R. Godine. "The Barracuda" by John Gardner from *A Child's Bestiary* published by Alfred A. Knopf. Copyright © 1977 by Boskydell Artists Ltd. Reprinted by permission of Georges Borchardt, Inc. on behalf of the estate of John Gardner.

Every effort has been made to trace all the copyright holders and the publishers apologize if any inadvertent omission has been made.

*With special thanks to Laura Cecil
for her invaluable help in compiling this collection.*

For Lily and Willoughby

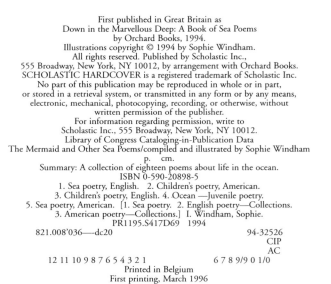

Library of Congress Cataloging-in-Publication Data
The Mermaid and Other Sea Poems/compiled and illustrated by Sophie Windham.
p. cm.
Summary: A collection of eighteen poems about life in the ocean.
ISBN 0-590-20898-5
1. Sea poetry, English. 2. Children's poetry, American.
3. Children's poetry, English. 4. Ocean —Juvenile poetry.
5. Sea poetry, American. [1. Sea poetry. 2. English poetry—Collections.
3. American poetry—Collections.] I. Windham, Sophie.
PR1195.S417D69 1994
821.008'036—-dc20   94-32526
                                                                     CIP
                                                                     AC
12 11 10 9 8 7 6 5 4 3 2 1   6 7 8 9/9 0 1/0
Printed in Belgium
First printing, March 1996

CONTENTS

THE SHARK

A treacherous monster is the Shark
He never makes the least remark.

And when he sees you on the sand,
He doesn't seem to want to land.

He watches you take off your clothes,
And not the least excitement shows.

His eyes do not grow bright or roll,
He has astounding self-control.

He waits till you are quite undressed,
And seems to take no interest.

And when towards the sea you leap,
He looks as if he were asleep.

But when you once get in his range,
His whole demeanor seems to change.

He throws his body right about,
And his true character comes out.

It's no use crying or appealing,
He seems to lose all decent feeling.

After this warning you will wish
To keep clear of this treacherous fish.

His back is black, his stomach white,
He has a very dangerous bite.

Lord Alfred Douglas

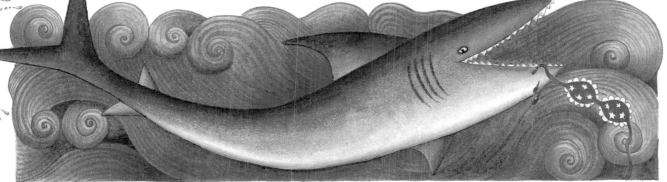

WHALE

Wouldn't you like to be a whale
And sail serenely by—
An eighty-foot whale from the tip of your tail
And a tiny, briny eye?
Wouldn't you like to wallow
Where nobody says "Come out!"?
  Wouldn't you *love* to swallow
  And blow all the brine about?
Wouldn't you like to be always clean
But never to have to wash, I mean,
And wouldn't you love to spout—
  O yes, just think—
A feather of spray as you sail away,
And rise and sink and rise and sink,
And blow all the brine about?

Geoffrey Dearmer

DO OYSTERS SNEEZE?

Do oysters sneeze beneath the seas,
or wiggle to and fro,
or sulk, or smile, or dance awhile
...how can we ever know?

Do oysters yawn when roused at dawn,
and do they ever weep,
and can we tell, when, in its shell,
an oyster is asleep?

Jack Prelutsky

SEAHORSE

O under the ocean waves
I gallop the seaweed lanes,
I jump the coral reef,
And all with no saddle or reins.

I haven't a flowing mane,
I've only this horsy face,
But under the ocean waves
I'm king of the steeplechase.

Blake Morrison

THE LOBSTER QUADRILLE

"Will you walk a little faster?" said a whiting to a snail.
"There's a porpoise close behind us, and he's treading on
    my tail.
See how eagerly the lobsters and the turtles all advance!
They are waiting on the shingle—will you come and join
    the dance?
    Will you, won't you, will you, won't you, will you join
      the dance?
    Will you, won't you, will you, won't you, won't you
      join the dance?"

"You can really have no notion how delightful it will be,
When they take us up and throw us, with the lobsters, out
    to sea!"
But the snail replied "Too far, too far!" and gave a look
    askance—
Said he thanked the whiting kindly, but he would not join
    the dance.
    Would not, could not, would not, could not, would not
      join the dance.
    Would not, could not, would not, could not, could not
      join the dance.

"What matters it how far we go?" his scaly friend replied.
"There is another shore, you know, upon the other side.
The further off from England the nearer is to France—
Then turn not pale, beloved snail, but come and join the
    dance.
  Will you, won't you, will you, won't you, will you join
    the dance?
  Will you, won't you, will you, won't you, won't you
    join the dance?"

Lewis Carroll

GRIM AND GLOOMY

Oh, grim and gloomy
So grim and gloomy
Are the caves beneath the sea.
Oh, rare but roomy
And bare and boomy,
Those salt sea caverns be.

Oh, slim and slimy
Or grey and grimy
Are the animals of the sea.
Salt and oozy
And safe and snoozy
The caves where those animals be.

Hark to the shuffling,
Huge and snuffling,
Ravenous, cavernous,
Great sea-beasts!
But fair and fabulous,
Tintinnabulous,
Gay and fabulous are their feasts.

Ah, but the queen of the sea,
The querulous, perilous sea!
How the curls of her tresses
The pearls on her dresses,
Sway and swirl in the waves,
How cozy and dozy,
How sweet ring-a-rosy
Her bower in the deep-sea caves.

Oh, rare but roomy
And bare and boomy
Those caverns under the sea,
And grave and grandiose,
Safe and sandiose
The dens of her denizens be.

James Reeves

THE BARRACUDA

Slowly, slowly, he cruises,

And slowly, slowly, he chooses

Which kind of fish he prefers to take this morning;

Then without warning

The Barracuda opens his jaws, teeth flashing,

And with a horrible, horrible grinding and gnashing,

Devours a hundred poor creatures and feels no remorse.

It's no wonder, of course,

That no little fish much likes the thing,

And indeed, it occasionally strikes the thing,

That he really ought, perhaps, to change his ways.

"But," (as he says

With an evil grin)

"It's actually not my fault, you see:

I've nothing to do with the tragedy;

I open my mouth for a yawn and—ah me!—

They all swim in."

John Gardner

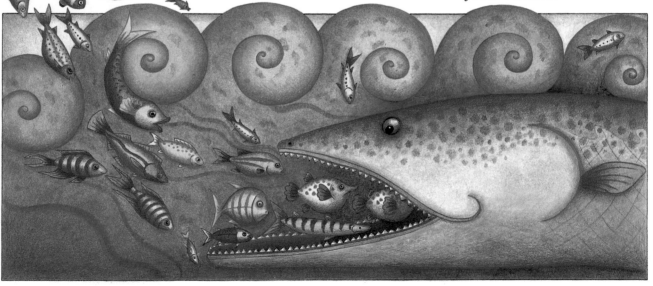

UNDERSEA

Beneath the waters
  Green and cool
The mermaids keep
  A swimming school.

The oysters trot;
  The lobsters prance;
The dolphins come
  To join the dance.

But the jellyfish
  Who are rather small
Can't seem to learn
  The steps at all

Marchette Chute

17

MY OTHER GRANNY

My Granny is an Octopus
   At the bottom of the sea,
And when she comes to supper
   She brings her family.

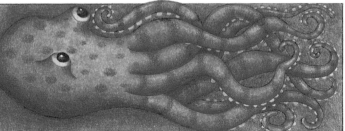

She chooses a wild wet windy night
   When the world rolls blind
As a boulder in the night-sea surf,
   And her family troops behind.

The sea-smell enters with them
   As they sidle and slither and spill
With their huge eyes and their tiny eyes
   And a dripping ocean-chill.

Some of her cousins are lobsters
   Some floppy jelly fish—
What would you be if your family tree
   Grew out of such a dish?

Her brothers are crabs jointed and knobbed
   With little pinhead eyes.
Their pincers crack the biscuits
   And they bubble joyful cries.

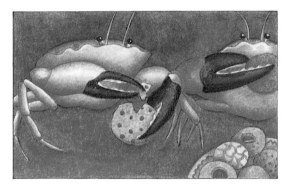

Crayfish the size of ponies
     Creak as they sip their milk.
My father stares in horror
     At my mother's secret ilk.

They wave long whiplash antennae,
     They sizzle and they squirt—
We smile and waggle our fingers back
     Or grandma would be hurt.

"What's new, Ma?" my father asks,
     "Down in the marvellous deep?"
Her face swells up, her eyes bulge huge
     And she begins to weep.

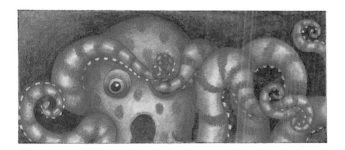

She knots her sucker tentacles
     And gapes like a nestling bird,
And her eyes flash, changing stations,
     As she attempts a WORD—

Then out of her eyes there brim two drops
     That plop into her saucer—
And that is all she manages,
     And my Dad knows he can't force her.

And when they've gone, my ocean-folk,
     No man could prove they came—
For the sea-tears in her saucer
     And a man's tears are the same.

Ted Hughes

THE MERMAID

Say not the mermaid is a myth,

I knew one once named Mrs. Smith.

She stood while playing cards or knitting:

Mermaids are not equipped for sitting.

Ogden Nash

THE EEL

I don't mind eels

Except as meals

And the way they feels.

Ogden Nash

OCEAN DINERS

They open up their beaks and throats
For breakfast off the backs of boats.

Some take a dip and dive for brunch,
Some join the passengers for lunch—

Or swoop in low for sneak attacks
On things like peanut butter snacks.

And when they're in a *hungry* mood,
Sea gulls love your finger food!

J. Patrick Lewis

THE DOLPHIN

On a beach in the morning
The sea green and blue
A young child was resting:
The same age as you.

From a spot near a towel
A whispering came
Like a rustle of leaves
Or a voice in a dream.

Where the ripples were circling
A dolphin appeared
And said, "Come down with me."
And then—DISappeared.

The child entered softly
And reached the sea-floor
And saw not a sign
Of the golden sea-shore.

There were molluscs in sea-shells
Anemones too,
And more fish than the child
Had observed in the zoo.

On the back of the dolphin
The child wished and watched
How the fish gather round
As the fish-eggs are hatched.

22

Fast and faster
The dolphin progressed
And they passed near to China
As they streaked from the West.

And then there were goldfish
As large as your knee,
And twenty-five pandas
Asleep by the sea.

In India fish had
The most wonderful marks
(But they missed out Australia
Because of the sharks).

At the end of the journey
They were back near the beach
When they talked of their trip
With bubbles for speech.

Then the child swam back strongly
To the spot on the sand
And covered up eyes
With a back of a hand.

In an hour the child woke up
In bed, it would seem.
Do you think that it happened
Or was it a dream?

Alan Bold

THERE WAS AN OLD PERSON OF HYDE

There was an Old Person of Hyde,

Who walked by the shore with his bride,

Till a Crab who came near, fill'd their bosoms with fear,

And they said, "Would we'd never left Hyde!"

Edward Lear

NARWHAL

Around their igloo fires with glee
  The Eskimos tell tales
Of Narwhal. Listen and you'll see
  This unicorn of whales
Through frosty waves off Greenland's coast
  Majestically advance.
And like a knight come forth to joust
  Hold high its wary lance.

X.J. Kennedy

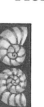

A SEA-SERPENT SAW
A BIG TANKER

A sea-serpent saw a big tanker,

Bit a hole in her side and then sank her.

It swallowed the crew

In a minute or two,

And then picked its teeth with the anchor.

Anonymous

THE FLATTERED FLYING FISH

Said the Shark to the Flying Fish over the phone:
"Will you join me tonight? I am dining alone.
Let me order a nice little dinner for two!
And come as you are, in your shimmering blue."

Said the Flying Fish: "Fancy remembering me,
And the dress that I wore at the Porpoises' tea!"
"How could I forget?" said the Shark in his guile:
"I expect you at eight!" and rang off with a smile.

She has powdered her nose; she has put on her things;
She is off with one flap of her luminous wings.
O little one, lovely, light-hearted and vain,
The Moon will not shine on your beauty again!

E.V. Rieu

SEAL LULLABY

Oh! hush thee, my baby, the night is behind us,
And black are the waters that sparkled so green.
The moon, o'er the combers, looks downward to find us
At rest in the hollows that rustle between.
Where billow meets billow, there soft be thy pillow;
Ah, weary wee flipperling, curl at thy ease!
The storm shall not wake thee, nor sharks overtake thee,
Asleep in the arms of the slow-swinging seas.

Rudyard Kipling

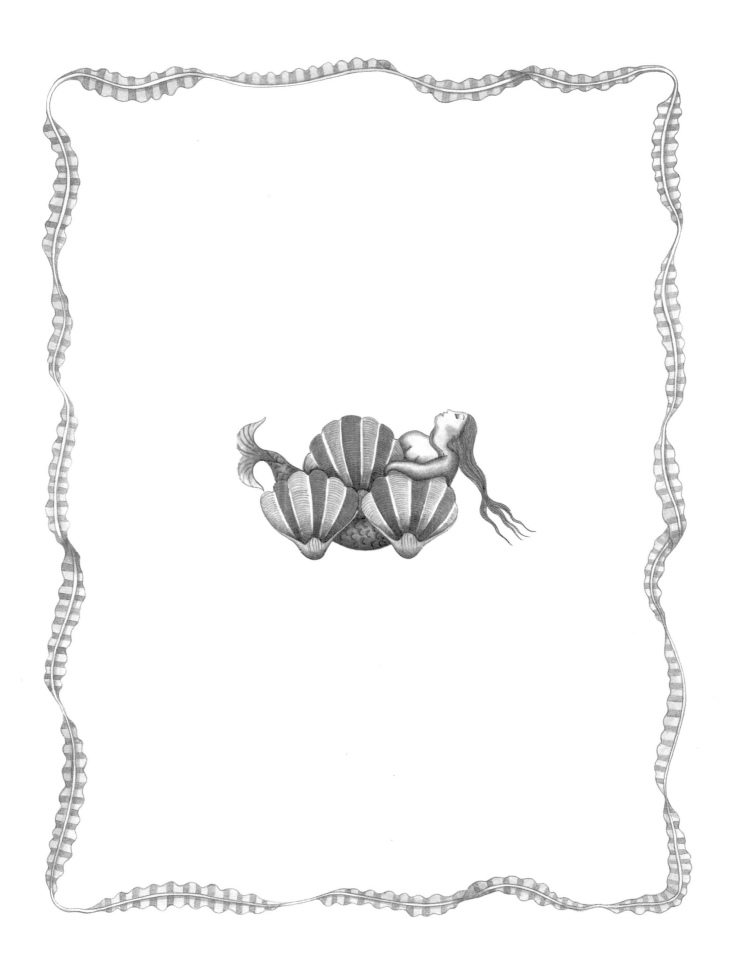